Hatching Chick

W9-AOD-471

Dona Herweck Rice

✳ Smithsonian

Contributing Author

Jennifer Lawson

Consultants

Jennifer Zoon
Communications Specialist
Smithsonian's National Zoo

Sharon Banks
3rd Grade Teacher
Duncan Public Schools

Publishing Credits

Rachelle Cracchiolo, M.S.Ed., *Publisher*
Conni Medina, M.A.Ed., *Managing Editor*
Diana Kenney, M.A.Ed., NBCT, *Content Director*
Véronique Bos, *Creative Director*
Robin Erickson, *Art Director*
Michelle Jovin, M.A., *Associate Editor*
Mindy Duits, *Senior Graphic Designer*
Smithsonian Science Education Center

Image Credits: front cover, p.1, pp.2–3, p.6, p.7 (all), p.14, p.17 (all), p.20, p.21, p.22 (bottom), p.24, p.25 (all) © Smithsonian; p.8 (bottom) Designua/Dreamstime; p.9 (bottom) The Photolibrary Wales/Alamy; p.10 Ashley Cooper pics/Alamy; p.11 Vince Burton/Alamy; p.13 ANT Photo Library/Science Source; p.23 (bottom) blickwinkel/Alamy; p.26 (bottom) Travelib Wales/Alamy; all other images from iStock and/or Shutterstock.

Library of Congress Cataloging-in-Publication Data

Names: Rice, Dona, author.
Title: Hatching a chick / Dona Herweck Rice.
Description: Huntington Beach, CA : Teacher Created Materials, [2019] |
    Audience: K to Grade 3. | Includes index. |
Identifiers: LCCN 2018030209 (print) | LCCN 2018034796 (ebook) | ISBN
    9781493869015 | ISBN 9781493866618
Subjects: LCSH: Birds--Conservation--Juvenile literature.
Classification: LCC QL676.5 (ebook) | LCC QL676.5 .R54 2020 (print) | DDC
    598.14/68--dc23

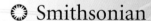

Teacher Created Materials

5301 Oceanus Drive
Huntington Beach, CA 92649-1030
www.tcmpub.com

ISBN 978-1-4938-6661-8

© 2019 Teacher Created Materials, Inc.
Printed in Malaysia
Thumbprints.21251

Table of Contents

3

Hello, World!

Pip! A tiny crack appears on a little brown egg. Inside the shell, a baby bird prepares to **hatch**. It knows by **instinct** how to free itself from its shell. Soon enough, it will stand on its own feet and breathe the fresh air of the outside world.

Welcome to the world, little chick!

A herring gull chick begins to hatch.

herring gull chick

Sometimes, birds need help with their eggs. Chicks do not need help breaking out of their shells. But some adult bird **species** may need help caring for their eggs in the first place.

Bird keepers help them. These scientists step in when bird species are **endangered**. They help some bird parents hatch and raise chicks so the chicks grow healthy and strong.

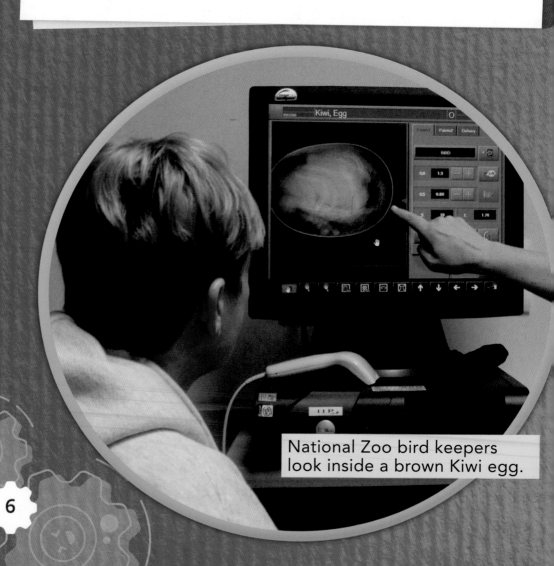

National Zoo bird keepers look inside a brown Kiwi egg.

This brown Kiwi is one day old.

This brown Kiwi hatched at Smithsonian's National Zoo.

How an Egg Hatches

To learn how bird keepers help, it is good to know how an egg hatches.

Just before a bird hatches, it **absorbs** egg yolk into its body. This will be its food for the first few hours or days outside the shell.

The bird also needs air. An air pocket forms at the top of the egg. The bird breathes this air just before it hatches.

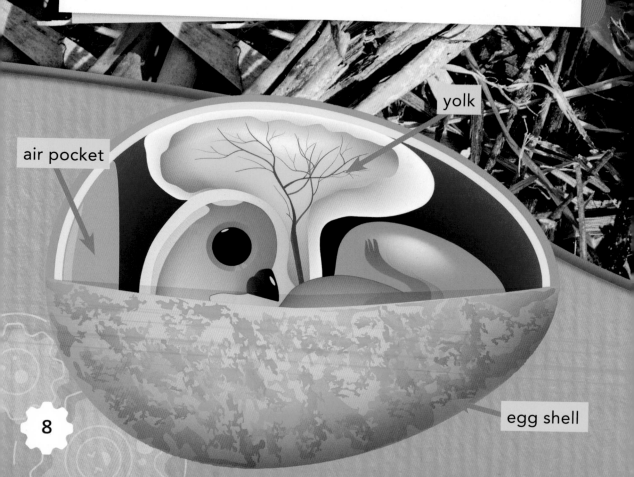

yolk

air pocket

egg shell

These gull chicks are at different stages of hatching.

Most of the time, people should not help baby birds break from their shells. They might hurt the baby birds.

The baby bird begins **pipping** from inside its shell. It uses a special horn-like bump, called an egg tooth, to crack the shell and break through. The egg tooth is a hard, white bump on its beak or jaw. For most birds, the egg tooth falls off a few days after the bird hatches.

At last, the bird uses its shoulders and legs to push up. It leaves the shell behind. It has hatched!

egg tooth

A gull chick rests on its egg.

egg tooth

pipping

A gull chick waits for another chick to pip from inside its shell.

What an Egg Needs

Baby birds grow inside their eggs for a set amount of time. That time depends on the species. Chickens **incubate** for three weeks. Emperor penguins take two months. A bird hatches when it fills the space inside the egg.

Time is different for each species. But what goes on inside the egg is much the same.

Arts

Egg-cellent Art

The outsides of eggs are just as cool as the insides! Each species lays eggs with its own patterns or colors. These designs are usually created a few hours before the eggs are laid. These designs may help them blend in with their nests.

An emperor penguin incubates an egg in a pouch above its feet.

Temperature

Healthy birds need the right temperature as they grow. That is why some bird parents may incubate their eggs. That means they keep their eggs warm with their bodies.

Bird keepers can help. They can place eggs in incubators. These machines make sure eggs stay at the right temperatures. They help birds grow and hatch well.

A National Zoo bird keeper places a Kiwi egg in an incubator.

A great flamingo incubates an egg by sitting on it.

Humidity

All life needs water. Humidity is water in the air. Eggs do well in the right humidity. Eggs also need it for their air pockets to grow.

Chicks inside eggs may die with too much or too little humidity. Bird keepers can control it, though. They use incubators to do so. Keepers watch both the temperature and humidity of eggs to make sure chicks are growing well.

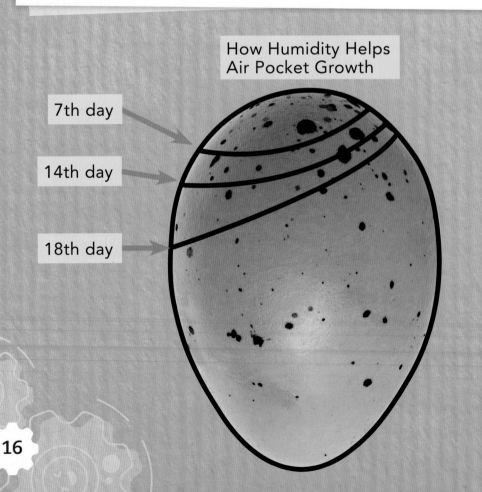

How Humidity Helps Air Pocket Growth

7th day

14th day

18th day

A National Zoo bird keeper candles an egg.

Technology & Engineering

Candling

Bird keepers use candling to check the health and growth of egg **embryos**. Keepers hold eggs to light sources, such as flashlights or candles. The light helps keepers see things inside eggs.

Rotation

Bird parents rotate their eggs while they incubate. They turn them often. This helps embryos grow as they should. Chicks may die if their eggs are not turned.

Eggs are curved so that birds can turn them easily, even without hands. But bird keepers can use their hands to turn eggs. Some incubators are also built to turn eggs.

A southern screamer uses her beak to rotate her egg.

southern screamer birds

Some eggs have a smaller end, so they usually roll in a circle. They do not easily roll out of their nests.

Egg Stories

Bird keepers have helped many at-risk species. Here are some of their stories.

Guam Rail Chicks

Guam rails were once thought to be **extinct**. Keepers at a zoo introduced a male and female. The birds got along! The female laid two eggs. Keepers helped the embryos grow and kept the chicks fed and safe. Once the chicks are old enough, they will be sent to live in the wild.

This Guam rail chick was one of the two chicks born at the zoo.

Smithsonian scientist Erica Royer releases a Guam rail into the wild.

Science

Watch Out!

Invasive species are plants or animals that do not belong in an area. Brown tree snakes are an invasive species. They endangered Guam rail chicks. Scientists had to remove them from Rota and Cocos Islands to keep the birds safe.

Loggerhead Shrikes

There were once a lot of loggerhead shrikes. Now, there are just a few left. Bird keepers are working to keep the species alive by taking adult birds into their care. They watch over the eggs, so they have a good chance of hatching. Then, they care for the chicks. Bird keepers feed them and keep them safe. They think their work will bring the birds back to the wild in large numbers.

This adult loggerhead shrike lives at the Smithsonian Conservation Biology Institute.

An adult loggerhead shrike feeds its chick.

Loggerhead shrikes eat insects and rodents.

White-Naped Cranes

White-naped cranes are at risk. One problem they are facing is that their **breeding grounds** are shrinking. So, fewer chicks are being born. When bird keepers found a healthy female crane not laying eggs, they knew they had to help.

Walnut the crane was raised by humans. She did not get along well with her species. But she bonded with a bird keeper! He uses science to help her lay healthy eggs. Now, she is a mother.

Walnut stands by the Smithsonian bird keeper she bonded with, Chris Crowe.

A white-naped crane checks on her chick.

white-naped crane chick

In the Numbers

When more members of a species die than are born, the species is dying out. Scientists try to find how many of each species is left. When species' numbers go down, scientists may need to help. It is unlikely the species will grow without help.

Hatching a Plan

There are many bird species that need help. It may not be possible to save them all. Bird keepers decide which species they can help the most. They work to protect the birds. They help those birds raise healthy chicks.

Bird keepers are not always successful. They cannot save all birds. Even so, they keep hatching new plans to help birds grow.

A bird keeper in Wales holds a great grey owl.

A bird keeper walks with Humboldt penguins.

STEAM CHALLENGE

Define the Problem

A bird egg has just fallen from its nest in a tree. It did not crack, but the parents are nowhere to be found. Use what you know about hatching eggs to create a new "nest." Your nest must keep the egg safe until bird keepers can take the egg.

Constraints: You may use any materials that could be found in various birds' nests, such as twine, yarn, or natural materials.

Criteria: A successful nest must have space to rotate the egg. Your nest should be able to hold a weighted plastic egg for one minute.

Research and Brainstorm

Why is it important to rotate an egg? What can bird keepers use to help eggs stay safe while still in the hatching process?

Design and Build

Sketch a design of your nest. What purpose will each part serve? What materials will work best? Build the model.

Test and Improve

Place a weighted plastic egg in your nest for one minute. Did it hold? Is there space for the egg to rotate? How can you improve it? Improve your design and try again.

Reflect and Share

How can your nest protect an egg? Are there other materials that would have been helpful in making your nest strong and safe?

Glossary

absorbs—takes in

breeding grounds— places where adult animals go to produce their young

embryos—animals or humans in the early stages of life before they are born or hatched

endangered— describes a type of animal or plant that is in danger of dying out completely

extinct—describes a type of animal or plant that has died out completely

hatch—to be born by coming out of an egg

incubate—sit on eggs so they will be kept warm and hatch

instinct—a way of behaving or thinking that is natural and does not need to be learned

pipping—cracking and breaking through an egg's shell

species—groups of animals or plants that are alike and can produce young together

Index

Do you want to be a bird keeper? Here are some tips to get you started.

"Watch animals without disturbing them. See how they act. This will help you learn what animals need and like." —*Chris Crowe, Animal Keeper*

"To be a great keeper, you need to love animals. It is hard work. But, it is a rewarding job knowing that you are teaching people about animals." —*Sara Hallager, Curator of Birds*

PICK A PARTY

The Big Book of Party Themes and Occasions

BY PATTY SACHS

Meadowbrook Press

Distributed by Simon & Schuster

New York

Publication Data

Sachs, Patty.
    Pick a party : the big book of party themes / Patty Sachs.
        p. cm.
    ISBN 0-88166-280-1
    1. Entertaining. I. Title.
GV1471.S19   1997
793.2—dc21   97-20080
                                                              CIP

Publisher's ISBN: 0-88166-280-1
Simon & Schuster Ordering # 0-671-52123-3

Editor: Liya Lev Oertel
Production Manager: Joe Gagne
Production Assistant: Danielle White
Cover Art: Jack Lindstrom

Published by Meadowbrook Press, 5451 Smetana Drive, Minnetonka, MN 55343

BOOK TRADE DISTRIBUTION by Simon & Schuster, a division of Simon and
Schuster, Inc., 1230 Avenue of the Americas, New York, NY 10020

00 99 98 97   10 9 8 7 6 5 4 3 2 1

Printed in the United States of America